My Son CHRISTOPHER

A 9/11 MOTHER'S TALE REMEMBRANCE

MAUREEN CRETHAN SANTORA

ILLUSTRATED BY
CHRISTOPHER ECHEVARRIA

Copyright © 2008, 2024 by Maureen Crethan Santora.

All rights reserved. No part of this book may be reproduced, stored, or transmitted by any means—whether auditory, graphic, mechanical, or electronic—without written permission of both publisher and author, except in the case of brief excerpts used in critical articles and reviews. Unauthorized reproduction of any part of this work is illegal and is punishable by law.

Library of Congress Control Number: 2008902596

ISBN: 979-8-89419-004-4 (sc)
ISBN: 979-8-89419-005-1 (hc)
ISBN: 979-8-89419-006-8 (e)

Because of the dynamic nature of the Internet, any web addresses or links contained in this book may have changed since publication and may no longer be valid. The views expressed in this work are solely those of the author and do not necessarily reflect the views of the publisher, and the publisher hereby disclaims any responsibility for them.

One Galleria Blvd., Suite 1900, Metairie, LA 70001
(504) 702-6708

This book is dedicated to all the mothers and fathers who have lost a son or daughter. Losing a child is one of the most painful experiences in life. The Pain is constantly with you. Parents love their children unconditionally for their entire lives. As survivors however we must help others remember what our son and daughters were like. We desperately want others to remember all of their special traits, their gifts as well as their faults. These are the things that make them special. As you remember your child know that others really understand your pain. We must never forget. God bless you in your journey toward healing.

Maureen Crethan Santora

Christopher's Mother

When a child is born there are celebrations. Parents are joyous and happy and most of all they love their new baby with all their hearts. When Christopher was born his father and I were filled with love and joy. He was special because he was our son. We loved him unconditionally.

When Christopher was little he loved to play with blocks. He loved to play with action figures. He loved playing with his friends in pretend imaginary action packed games. He loved making mess. He loved to play. He was like most boys who loved to play and make a mess but, he was special because he was my son.

Christopher wanted to go to school like his older sisters, Jennifer and Patricia. He went to Nursery School when he was three years old. He loved being in school. The teachers told us that he loved to play and have fun and that sometimes he didn't follow all the rules. He was like many children who loved to play and have fun and sometimes didn't follow all the rules but, he was special because he was my son.

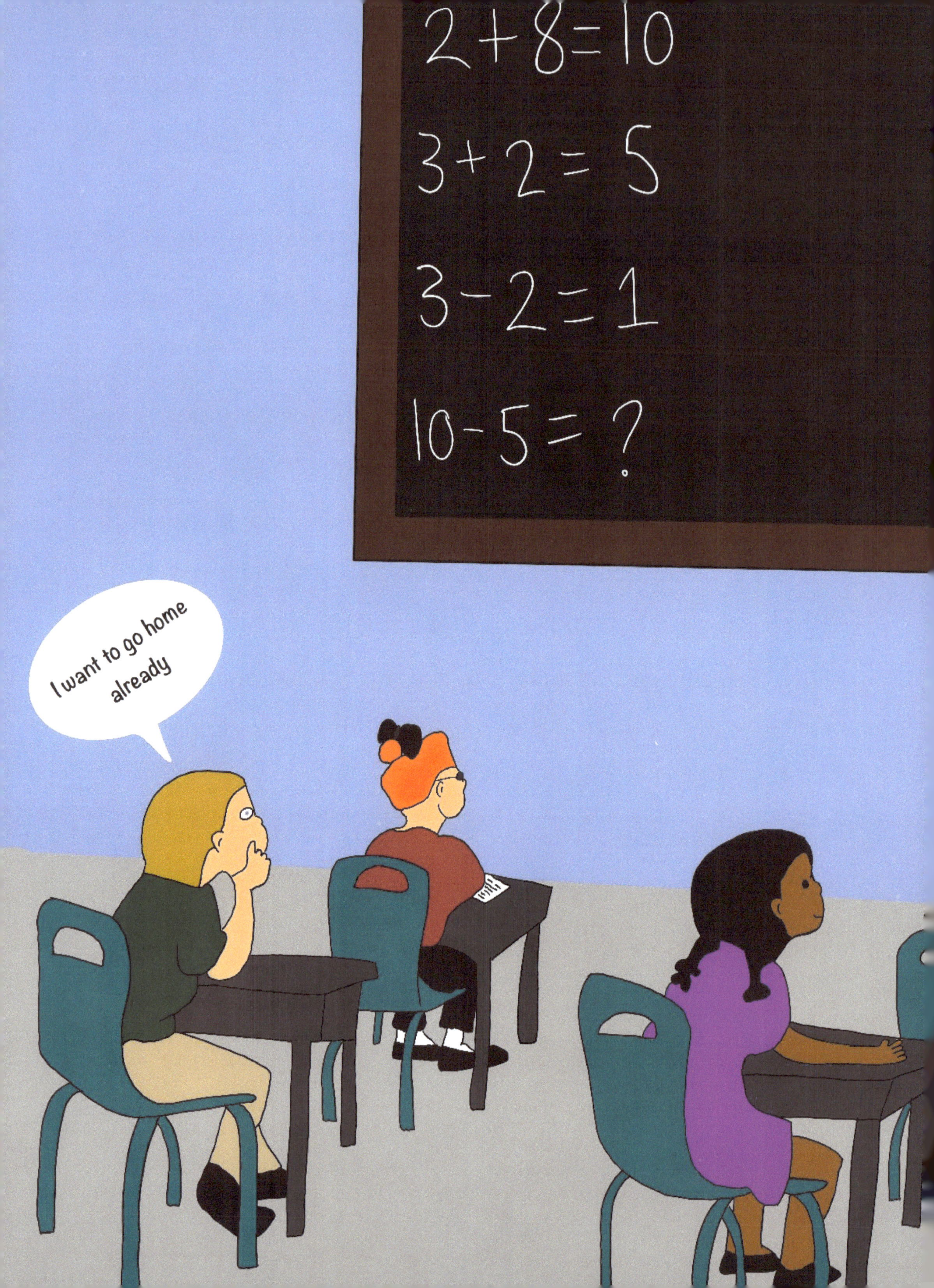
2+8=10
3+2=5
3-2=1
10-5=?
I want to go home already

Christopher went to elementary school. He said that school was boring. He wanted to talk and play and have fun. School was not always fun. He had to follow rules and wait his turn and listen to adults. He was like many other students who had to follow rules and wait for their turn and listen to adults but, he was special because he was my son.

When Christopher went to middle school he learned to play the clarinet. He sometimes gave his teachers a hard time. Often he got into trouble because he didn't want to do what the teachers told him to do. He was smart and quick and sometimes he had to wait for another student to "catch on." He was like many other quick students who had to wait for other students to "catch on" but, he was special because he was my son.

In high school, Christopher was in the Band and the Orchestra. He quickly learned that being in honors classes gave him the opportunity to speak his mind. Christopher still liked to play. He played basketball everyday after school. He loved sports. He played tennis. He swam and became a lifeguard. He spoke his mind at every opportunity. He loved jokes. He was special however, because he was my son.

After high school Christopher went to college. He majored in History. Christopher still loved facts. He loved American History and Ancient History. He read about many heroes like William Wallace and Paul Revere. He admired people who stood up for their beliefs and fought for freedom. He had many friends. All were smart and loved sports. All were opinionated and vocal about their beliefs. Christopher was special though, because he was my son.

When Christopher graduated from college he became a teacher. He loved teaching. He taught in elementary school and in middle school. Each time he taught he included some American History. Christopher loved American History. He talked about heroes. He talked about dreams. Christopher felt that everyone should follow his dream. Christopher's dream was to become a firefighter like his father. Christopher was still very special because he was my son.

In February of 2001, Christopher became a firefighter. He left teaching and followed his dream. Christopher was very proud to be a firefighter. Firefighters were heroes. Firefighters were brave. Firefighters helped people and saved lives. Christopher wanted to be a good firefighter. He wanted to help people. He wanted to save lives. I was very proud of Christopher because he was following his dream. He had always been special because he was my son.

On September 11, 2001 my son Christopher lost his life. He had always been special because he was my son. Now he was special because he was one of the 343 firefighters who gave his life helping others. He was part of a special group of heroes that will forever be part of history. On that day thousands of people were saved because of people like Christopher and his 342 firefighter brothers who risked and gave their lives to help others. We can never bring them back or adequately thank the families for their sacrifice. We can only say thank you to all those like Christopher and his firefighting brothers.

Christopher will always be special because he was my son. He will always be with me in my heart. He will always be a part of his sisters' lives in their hearts and memories. Kathleen his youngest sister joined the Army to fight for freedom. None of us will ever be the same. All the other families feel the same way about their sons, daughters, and husbands, wives, fathers, mothers, sisters, brothers and all the other relatives who lost their lives on that hate filled day.

How can we honor all these victims? What can we do? We can remember that hatred is a terrible thing. We can work hard not to hate anyone ourselves. We can remember all the fun we had with these heroes. We can help others remember too. We can live our lives honoring our heroes. In this way all the "Christophers" who died on that horrible day will be special like my son Christopher who will be special forever in my heart and my mind and my soul.

We must always remember September 11, 2001. We must remember what hatred can do. We must work hard to respect each other and be tolerant of others. We must forgive and most of all we must tell the people we love that we love them each and every day.

SPECIAL MEMORIALS TO CHRISTOPHER SANTORA

Like most September 11, 2001 families, Christopher's family wanted everyone to remember him in a special way. So did members of his community. To honor him, Christopher's family established a special scholarship fund in his honor. The scholarship fund gives college scholarships and grants to schools in all levels: elementary, middle and high schools. College scholarships are given through out the country. In addition college scholarships are given to the children of firefighters in New York City. Our annual basketball game was eliminated because of COVID. It ran for many years. Christopher loved to play basketball more than any other sport. It was called "For the Love of the Game" and was open to everyone. Participants received special shirts and trophies. For more information you can go to: http://www.Santorafund.org.

A street was named after Firefighter Christopher A Santora. It is located on 33 Road in Astoria, Queens, New York.

A school, P.S. 222 was named after Firefighter Christopher A. Santora. It is called the Firefigher Christopher A. Santora Early Childhood School. It is located in Jackson Heights, Queens, New York. It was opened in September 2002. At the time it was the only school that was named after a firefighter from September 11, 2001. Since then, a few more schools have been named after firefighters and people who died on September 11, 2001. Christopher's school was the first however. Students who attend are in Pre Kindergarten to grade 2 classes. Christopher's uniform and toys and books are in a special cabinet in the lobby of the school.

A basketball court was dedicated to Christopher. It is located behind Christopher's home in Astoria, Queens. This is the basketball court where Christopher played every day after he did his homework.

A playground was dedicated to Christopher. It is located in Tafton, Pennsylvania. It was re-dedicated in the Fall of 2023. Christopher played in this playground when he was little.

A book was written entitled "The Day the Towers Fell." It is the story of September 11, 2001. It was dedicated to Christopher.

And, finally, this book was written so that students around the world would learn about "My Son Christopher."

Christopher
Nursery School

Christopher
Grade 1

Christopher with his parents, nana,
and sisters; Jennifer (L) & Patricia (R)

Christopher with nana, Patricia (L),
and Jennifer (R)

Graduation day
Christopher, Jennifer, Megan, Patricia, and Kathleen

High School Picture

Christopher
1st Communion, Grade 2

Christopher and Grandmummy
High School Graduation, June 1994

Christopher in
Greece, April 1996

A Favorite picture of Christopher with his favorite character TIGGER

Christopher's High School Graduation, June 1994

College Graduation ceremony (Queens College) June 2000
John (Patricia's Husband), Christopher, Patricia (2nd oldest sister).
On extreme right, Grand mummy (in a wheelchair)

Christopher with Gramps on his 90th birthday, August 2001

Christopher Graduation Day, FDNY, June 2001

Firefighter Christopher A. Santora in bunker gear

Firefighter Christopher A. Santora in dress uniform.

Students and children: Always remember that your parents will always love you no matter what. They must set rules to help you to be successful in life. That is their job. To love you unconditionally and take care of you.

Parents: Tell you children that you love them each and every day. Let them know how much you care about them.

www.ingramcontent.com/pod-product-compliance
Lightning Source LLC
LaVergne TN
LVHW070441070526
838199LV00036B/679